Tongues

by
Doug Batchelor

An Amazing Fact:

Legend has it that when the Greeks were unable to capture the city of Troy even after imposing a 10-year siege, they finally resorted to a clever stratagem. The Greek army pretended to sail away and left on the shore a huge, hollow wooden horse as an apparent victory gift. However, the gift was actually filled with several armed warriors! Sinon, a Greek spy inside Troy, persuaded the Trojans to bring the horse within the city walls, saying that to do so would mysteriously make Troy invincible. That night Sinon released the troops hiding in the gigantic horse. After killing the Trojan guards, they opened the gates to the waiting Greek soldiers, and Troy was captured and burned.

CHAPTER ONE

DIFFERENCES IN INTERPRETATION

A gift from an enemy can be very deadly. The underworld has successfully dispatched many human targets by beautifully wrapping a bomb as a gift with an ornate bow and paper that explodes when opened. Today the devil is using a counterfeit gift of the Spirit—a pagan form of the gift of tongues—to gain access to the church of God and destroy it from within.

Shortly after becoming a Christian, I was hitchhiking from Palm Springs to Los Angeles to visit my mother. About halfway to my destination, I caught a ride with a kind, middle-aged Pentecostal lady who was very pleased to hear of my recent conversion. As we drove along, she asked, "Have you received the Holy Ghost yet?"

I was a little surprised by her question, because no one had ever asked me that before. "Well, I think I have," I said slowly. "I've certainly felt God's Spirit in my life. The Lord is helping me make so many changes—you know, like giving up drugs, stealing, lying, cursing, and much more."

"No, that's not what I mean," she said, looking a little frustrated. "Have you received the baptism of the Holy Ghost? Do you speak in tongues?"

It struck me as odd that she seemed far more interested in whether or not I had experienced an ecstatic utterance than she was in the fact that I was having victory over the sins that had long held me captive!

Even still, this kind lady was convinced that I was missing out on a primary element of the Christian experience. And not wanting to be deprived of something so important, I began a very deep search into the controversial subject of tongues. The first few churches I attended were all charismatic, which means they believed in speaking in ecstatic tongues—an experience often described as "glossolalia." Most of my new friends at our Bible study group "spoke in tongues," so the information I am about to share is the result of firsthand experience as well as years of research.

I need to address some unpopular facts in this study, and I must begin by saying that although I disagree with some of the teachings of my charismatic brothers and sisters, I firmly believe that God has thousands of His children in these fellowships. I also recognize that even among charismatics there are vast differences of interpretation regarding the gift of tongues, so forgive me if I generalize at times. The war I wage is not against people, but against error. The same truth that at times can hurt will also promise to set us free (John 8:32)!

CHAPTER TWO

THE GENUINE GIFT OF TONGUES

L et's begin with a definition. The word "tongue" in the Bible simply means "a language."

God gives all the gifts of the Spirit to fill a practical need. What was the need for tongues?

Jesus told His followers, "Go ye therefore, and teach all nations, baptizing them in the name of the Father, and of the Son, and of the Holy Ghost" (Matthew 28:19). This command posed a problem. How could the apostles go out preaching to all the world when they spoke only one or two languages? After all, Jesus' disciples were very bright, even though most of them were not formally educated. In order to fulfill the great commission, He promised to give them a unique gift from the Holy Spirit.

It was a miraculous, supernatural ability to speak foreign languages they had not formerly studied or known for the purpose of spreading the Gospel.

"And these signs shall follow them that believe; … they shall speak with new tongues" (Mark 16:17).

The fact that Jesus said these new tongues, or languages, would be a "sign" indicates that the ability to speak them would not come as the result of normal linguistic study. Rather, it would be an instantaneous gift to fluently preach in a previously unfamiliar language.

There are only three actual examples of speaking in tongues recorded in the Bible (Acts chapters 2, 10, and 19). If we look at these three cases, we should find a clearer picture of this controversial gift.

"When the day of Pentecost was fully come, they were all with one accord in one place. And suddenly there came a sound from heaven as of a rushing mighty wind, and it filled all the house where they were sitting. And there appeared unto them cloven [divided] tongues like as of fire, and it sat upon each of them. And they were all filled with the Holy Ghost, and began to speak with other tongues, as the Spirit gave them utterance (Acts 2:1–4).

Fire is a symbol for power. God sent this gift in the form of tongues of fire so they would know that He would empower their feeble tongues in the same way He strengthened Moses to go before Pharaoh (Exodus 4:10–12) and touched Isaiah's lips with a coal from the heavenly altar (Isaiah 6:6, 7).

Why did the Lord wait until Pentecost to bestow this gift? Acts 2:5–11 sets the scene: "And there were dwelling at Jerusalem Jews, devout men, out of every nation under heaven. Now when this was noised abroad, the multitude came together, and were confounded, because that every man heard them speak in his own language. And they were all amazed and marvelled, saying one to another, Behold, are not all these which speak Galilaeans? And how hear we every man in our own tongue, wherein we were born? … We do hear them speak in our tongues the wonderful works of God."

The day of Pentecost was a Jewish holy day that fell 50 days after Passover. Devoted

Israelites would come from all over the Roman empire to worship in Jerusalem. God chose this timely opportunity to bestow this gift of tongues upon the disciples so they could preach to the visiting Jews in their native languages. At least 15 different language groups were represented in the crowd that day (Acts 2:9–11)! As a result, thousands of these visitors were converted. Then, after Pentecost, they in turn carried their new faith home to their respective countries.

From this example, it should be very clear that the gift of tongues was given to communicate the gospel in different existing languages of the world.

Some have mistakenly suggested that the miracle on Pentecost was a gift to hear and understand different languages. It was not a gift of hearing given to the listeners, but rather a gift of the Spirit given to enable the believers to speak (Acts 2:4). It is not called the gift of ears for the listeners, but the gift of tongues for the speakers. Furthermore, the sign was not ears of fire on the listeners, but tongues of fire on the ones preaching.

It is also sometimes suggested that the gift of tongues is a "heavenly language" understood only by God or those with the gift of interpretation. The Bible is clear in Acts chapter 2 that both the disciples and those listening understood what was being preached—"the wonderful works of God" (verse 11).

Let's look now at the second example when Peter preached to Cornelius and his household: "While Peter yet spake these words, the Holy Ghost fell on all them which heard the word. And they of the circumcision which believed were astonished, as many as came with Peter, because that on the Gentiles also was poured out the gift of the Holy Ghost. For they heard them speak with tongues, and magnify God" (Acts 10:44–46).

Acts 10:1 tells us that Cornelius was Italian, while Peter was a Jew and spoke Aramaic. History also tells us that the servants in a Roman home could be from anywhere in the world. Because there were obvious language barriers at this meeting, Peter likely began to preach through an interpreter. But when the Holy Ghost fell upon Cornelius and his household, the Jews with

Peter could understand the Gentiles speaking in languages other than their native tongues. The record is that the Jews heard them "magnify God" in these languages. When later reporting this experience to the church leaders, Peter said, "The Holy Ghost fell on them, *as on us at the beginning*" (Acts 11:15, emphasis added).

Peter here plainly tells us that Cornelius and his family received the same gift of tongues in the same way the disciples did on the day of Pentecost. In other words, they spoke languages they had not formerly known in a way that could be understood.

The third and final example of speaking in tongues is when Paul preached to 12 Ephesian disciples. Acts 19:6 records, "And when Paul had laid his hands upon them, the Holy Ghost came on them; and they spake with tongues, and prophesied."

Paul was the most educated and widely traveled of the apostles, and he spoke many languages (1 Corinthians 14:18). When the Holy Spirit came upon these 12 Ephesian men, Paul recognized that they were prophesying, or preaching, in new languages. Most likely, they spoke in languages common throughout the Roman Empire, since that would be practical for spreading the Gospel. Luke does not say that they received a form of tongues different from the first two examples, so we must assume that it was the same type of gift given at Pentecost.

You'll find that the only times the gift of tongues was associated with the outpouring of the Holy Spirit is when people from more than one language group were gathered together, thus creating communication barriers.

Notice that in Acts chapter 4 you have a repeat of the experience described in chapter 2. The place was shaken and they were filled with the Holy Spirit, but because there were no foreigners present, the gift of tongues was absent. Acts 4:31 says, "And when they had prayed, the place was shaken where they were assembled together; and they were all filled with the Holy Ghost, and they spake the word of God with boldness."

The purpose for the baptism of the Holy Spirit is not to mutter or babble unintelligible sounds, but rather to have power for preaching.

This is why Jesus said, "But ye shall receive power, after that the Holy Ghost is come upon you: and ye shall be witnesses unto me both in Jerusalem, and in all Judaea, and in Samaria, and unto the uttermost part of the earth" (Acts 1:8).

CHAPTER THREE
THE MESSAGE TO CORINTH

Of the 14 New Testament books written by Paul, 1 Corinthians is the only one in which he deals with the subject of tongues. The Corinthian church obviously had a specific, temporary problem because Paul's second letter to Corinth never even mentions tongues.

The ancient city of Corinth was famous for its two international seaports. Because the Corinthian church was a melting pot of many different nationalities, its services often became chaotic and confusing. Evidently some of the members would pray, testify, or preach in languages unknown to the others present. This is why Paul commanded that if they spoke in a tongue unknown to the majority, they should remain silent unless there was someone there to interpret or translate (1 Corinthians 14:28). In other words, it's not polite to speak in a language that your audience cannot understand. Listen to these plain statements from the apostle: "Now, brethren, if I come unto you speaking with tongues, what shall I profit you, except I shall speak to you either by revelation, or by knowledge, or by prophesying, or by doctrine? And even things without life giving sound, whether pipe or harp, except they give a distinction in the sounds, how shall it be known what is piped or harped? For if the trumpet give an uncertain sound, who shall prepare himself to the battle? So likewise ye, except ye utter by the tongue words easy to be understood, how shall it be known what is spoken? for ye shall speak into the air. ... Yet in the church I had rather speak five words with my understanding, that by my voice I might teach others also, than ten thousand words in an unknown tongue. ... If any man speak in an unknown tongue, let it be by two, or at the most by three, and that by course; and let one interpret. But if there be no interpreter, let him keep silence in the church;

and let him speak to himself, and to God" (1 Corinthians 14:6–9, 19, 27, 28).

It is truly amazing that some people take this passage and use it as an excuse to babble during services! The consistent message of Paul throughout Scripture is the very opposite. In 1 Timothy 6:20, he specifically mentions "avoiding profane and vain babblings." And in 2 Timothy 2:16, Paul repeats that counsel: "But shun profane and vain babblings: for they will increase unto more ungodliness." In other words, the very purpose for the gift of speech is to communicate your thoughts. If those present do not understand your communication, then keep silent.

CHAPTER FOUR
HEAVENLY PRAYER LANGUAGE?

Many of my charismatic friends would agree that the tongues spoken in the book of Acts were normal languages of the world. But they quickly add that there is a second gift—a heavenly prayer language. This gift, they say, is to express the Spirit's "groanings which cannot be uttered" (Romans 8:26). The purpose, they say, is so the devil cannot understand our prayers. But nowhere are we taught to hide our prayers from the devil. He trembles when he hears Christians pray!

This doctrine of a prayer language is based mainly upon 1 Corinthians 14:14, where Paul says, "For if I pray in an unknown tongue, my spirit prayeth, but my understanding is unfruitful."

They interpret this to mean that when Paul prayed in the Spirit, he used a "heavenly tongue" and did not himself know what he was praying. This theory raises an important question. How would the supplicant ever know if his prayer was answered?

So what is it that Paul is really saying here in 1 Corinthians 14:14? The problem in understanding this verse comes largely from the cumbersome translation. Please allow me to rephrase the verse in modern English: "If I pray in a language those around me do not know, I might be praying with the Spirit, but my thoughts would be unfruitful for those listening." Paul is adamant that if we pray out loud, we should either pray so others around us can understand or else keep quiet! Notice the next few verses: "What is it then? I will pray with the spirit, and I will pray with the understanding also: I will sing with the spirit, and I will sing with the understanding also. Else when thou shalt bless with the spirit, how shall he that occupieth the room of the unlearned say Amen at thy giving of thanks, seeing he understandeth not what thou sayest" (1 Corinthians 14:15, 16)? According to this text, who has the problem with understanding? It is the listener and not the speaker as is commonly taught. If you have ever prayed with someone who is offering a prayer in a language unknown to you, then you know what Paul meant when he said it is difficult for you to say "Amen" (meaning "so be it") at the end of the prayer. Without an interpreter, you have no idea to what you are assenting. You may have just asked a blessing on the devil as far as you can tell!

It is very obvious from the context of 1 Corinthians 14 that the purpose of speaking in tongues, or foreign languages, is to communicate the gospel and thereby edify the church. If the listeners do not understand the spoken language they cannot be edified. Consequently, if there is no interpreter, the speaker is simply speaking into the air and the only ones present who know what is being said are God and himself. This is the clear meaning of the often-misquoted verse 2. "For he that speaketh in an unknown tongue speaketh not unto men, but unto God: for no man understandeth him; howbeit in the spirit he speaketh mysteries."

Paul emphasizes again that the languages spoken need to be understood by the hearers or else the one who wants to share the mysteries of the gospel needs to sit quietly in meditation between himself and God. "So likewise ye; except ye utter by tongue words easy to be understood, how shall it be known what is spoken? for ye shall speak into the air." "But if there be no interpreter, let him keep silence in the church; and let him speak to himself, and to God" (verses 9, 28). Clearly, the entire purpose of tongues is to cross language barriers and communicate the gospel!

Some have asked, "Didn't Paul say he spoke with the tongues of angels?"

No. Paul said, *"Though* I speak with the tongues of men and of angels ..."* (1 Corinthians 13:1, emphasis added). If you read this verse in its context, you will see that the word "though" means "even if." For example, Paul also said in verse 2, *"Though* I have all faith ..."* He did not have all faith. And verse 3 adds, *"Though* I give my body to be burned ..."* Paul was beheaded, not burned. So we can see that Paul here used the word "though" to mean "even if."

CHAPTER FIVE
RIGHT PRIORITIES

I believe that all the gifts of the Spirit, including the true gift of tongues, are needed and available to the church today. But the Scriptures teach that some of the gifts are more important than others and that we should focus on the most important ones. "But covet earnestly the best gifts" (1 Corinthians 12:31).

In fact, when the Bible lists spiritual gifts, tongues is usually found at the bottom of the list. "And God hath set some in the church, first apostles, secondarily prophets, thirdly teachers, after that miracles, then gifts of healings, helps, governments, diversities of tongues" (1 Corinthians 12:28). "Greater is he that prophesieth than he that speaketh with tongues" (1 Corinthians 14:5).

Yet some charismatic preachers have turned the list upside down and made the gift of tongues the primary emphasis of their preaching. They would have us think that a Christian who does not speak in tongues is a second-class citizen. But Paul makes it clear that different gifts are given to different people, and no one is expected to have all the gifts. He asks in 1 Corinthians 12:29, 30: "Are all apostles? are all prophets? are all teachers? are all workers of miracles? Have all the gifts of healing? do all speak with tongues? do all interpret?" The answer is obviously NO!

The Bible says, "The fruit of the Spirit is love, joy, peace, longsuffering, gentleness, goodness, faith, Meekness, temperance" (Galatians 5:22, 23). But these same preachers would have us believe that the fruit of the Spirit is tongues or that every person who is filled with the Holy Spirit will speak in tongues. Yet out of more than 50 examples in the Bible where God filled His people with the Spirit, only three times is tongues connected with the experience.

Furthermore, Jesus is our example. He was filled with the Holy Spirit, yet He never spoke in tongues. John the Baptist was "filled with the Holy Ghost, even from his mother's womb" (Luke 1:15), but there is no record that he spoke in tongues, either.

Of the 27 books in the New Testament, only three make any reference at all to the gift of tongues. There are about 39 Bible authors. Of the 39, only three—Luke, Paul, and Mark—mention the subject of tongues. In other words, we should put the emphasis where God puts the emphasis.

CHAPTER SIX
CREATIVE COUNTERFEIT

The genuine gift of tongues is a powerful tool for the proclamation of the gospel. But remember, the devil has a counter̶ truth of God.

Glossolalia (glô´se-lå´lê-a) is the used to describe the popular experie̶ ̶c̶e found in most charismatic churches. It is defined in the *American Heritage Dictionary* as: "fabricated and non-meaningful speech, especially such speech associated with a trance state or certain schizophrenic syndromes."

Contrast that with the same dictionary's definition for a language: "The use by human beings of voice sounds, and often written symbols representing these sounds, in organized combinations and patterns in order to express and communicate thoughts and feelings." By any definition, the disjointed sounds of glossolalia are not a language.

Believe me, I have seen this practice many times. In one charismatic church I used to attend, the pastor and his wife were a "tongues team." Every week in the middle of the pastor's sermon, his wife would jump to her feet, throw her arms in the air, and break out in ecstatic utterance. But she always said the same thing.

...nda kala shami, handa kala shami, handa kala shami ..." Over and over again. This instantly seemed suspicious to me because Jesus said, "But when ye pray, use not vain repetitions, as the heathen do" (Matthew 6:7).

Each time this happened, the woman's husband would stop preaching and provide a dubious English translation for her so-called message. Usually it began with "Thus saith the Lord." Yet in spite of the fact that she always repeated the words "handa kala shami," the pastor's vague interpretation was different each time—and sometimes three times longer than the utterance. I used to wonder why, if this was a message from God, wouldn't He give it to us in English the first time.

CHAPTER SEVEN
BAPTIZED PAGANISM

My exposure to this charismatic "tongues team" reminded me of some things I had read in my history books growing up. This modern manifestation of tongues finds its roots not in the Bible, but rather in ancient pagan spiritualistic rituals. In the sixth century B.C., the Oracle of Delphi was housed in a temple built near the foot of Mt. Parnassus. Delphi was also sacred to Dionysus, the god associated with wine, fertility, and sensual dance, and to the nine Muses, patron goddesses of music.

While exhilarating music was played, Pythia, the chief priestess, would breathe intoxicating vapors, go into a frenzied trance, and then begin jabbering. The weird sounds the priestess muttered were then interpreted by a priest, who usually spoke in verse. Her utterances were regarded as the words of Apollo, but the messages were so ambiguous that they could seldom be proven wrong. [1]

While living with the Native Americans in New Mexico, I witnessed a similar ritual several times. The Indians would eat the hallucinogenic peyote, then sit in a circle and chant and pound drums for hours. Before long, several were spasmodically muttering as they experienced their tormenting visions. Today the charismatic churches are by far the most popular among the Native Americans because it is such an easy and natural transition from their old religions.

Among many heathen African tribes, in order to invoke the blessing of their gods, the people would sacrifice a chicken or goat and then dance around a fire for long hours, chanting songs to the hypnotic rhythm of a pounding drum. Eventually some of the people would become possessed by their gods and begin speaking the eerie languages of the spirit world. Then the local witch doctor or priest would translate the messages. This ritual is still practiced today among the Voodoo Catholics in the West Indies.

This pagan practice first found its way into the North American Christian churches in the early 1800s. Many of the African slaves who were brought to America and forced to accept Christianity were unable to read the Bible for themselves. Even though they came from a variety of tribes in Africa, one practice most tribes held in common was the "Spirit Dances" with the "spirit-possessed" person muttering.

The slaves mistakenly associated this with the Christian "gift of tongues" and began to incorporate a modified version into their meetings. These frantic services, which were accompanied by heavy rhythmic music, began to spread at first only in the South and the participants were mocked by the mainline denominations as "Holy Rollers." Some even went so far as to grab venomous serpents during their possessed trances as a means of proving that they had the "spirit." (This was a misuse of Mark 16:18, which says, "They shall take up serpents," in reference to the time Paul was accidentally bitten by a serpent but was unharmed by the venom. See Acts 28:3–6.) For people to hunt down and pick up deadly snakes in order to prove that they have the Holy Spirit is, in reality, tempting God!

The national expansion of the Pentecostal movement among Caucasians began in Los Angeles at the Apostolic Faith Gospel Mission on Azusa Street in 1906. The leader was a black former holiness preacher named William Seymour. From there, leaders continued to refine the doctrines and make them more attractive and palatable to other mainline Christians.

"Then in about 1960 the charismatic movement began attracting followers within traditional denominations. From then it continued to have explosive growth until now there are several million charismatics in Protestant and Catholic churches throughout the world." [2]

It is important to note the prominent role music plays in all the pagan religions that practice glossolalia. This counterfeit gift of tongues first found its foothold in mainline churches through "baptized" pagan music and worship styles. The dominant, repetitious rhythms and syncopated beat disarm the higher reasoning powers and put the subconscious mind in a hypnotic state. In this vulnerable condition, the spirit of ecstatic utterance finds easy access.

Now the devil is using this counterfeit gift of tongues, like a Trojan horse, to introduce pagan worship styles into Christian churches with a frightening degree of success. Satan wants to shift the attention of Christians from faith to feeling. Some of these charismatic churches go so far as to say that the Bible is the old letter, and that messages which come through tongues are fresh revelations of the Spirit and therefore more dependable.

So now the stage is set for Satan's final performance!

CHAPTER EIGHT
HOW GOD'S SPIRIT AFFECTS US

The concept that a person who is "slain in the spirit" should fall to the ground and wallow and mutter is an insult to the Holy Ghost. The reason God gives us His Spirit is to restore in us His image—not to rob us of all dignity and self control!

On Mount Carmel, the pagan prophets of Baal jumped on the altar and shouted and moaned. They prophesied and cut themselves. By contrast, Elijah quietly knelt and prayed a simple prayer (1 Kings 18:17–46).

"For God is not the author of confusion" (1 Corinthians 14:33). If God is not responsible, then who is?

The idea that we lose control when we receive the Spirit is not consistent with Scripture.

"The spirits of the prophets are subject to the prophets" (1 Corinthians 14:32).

Here's another case in point. After Jesus saved a berserk, demon-possessed man by the sea, the healed man was seen "sitting at the feet of Jesus, clothed, and in his right mind" (Luke 8:35). The invitation of God is "Come now, and let us reason together, saith the LORD" (Isaiah 1:18). He wants us to use our heads.

Some of you reading this study are no doubt thinking: "How dare you say these things? I have spoken in tongues for years and know it is from God!" As Christians, we should never base our conclusions on how we feel. After all, the devil can certainly make us feel good. Rather, we must base our beliefs upon the sure Word of God.

A friend of mine was an active charismatic who often spoke in tongues. When he studied these things, he began to question if this "gift" was from the right spirit. So he sincerely prayed and said, "Lord, if this is not Your will and if I am not experiencing the true gift of tongues, then please take it away!" He told me that from that day on, the experience of glossolalia never returned. A true Christian should be willing to surrender every cherished view and practice on the altar of God's will and forsake any practice that may be questionable—no matter how popular, accepted, or beloved among other Christians. There are some things that are highly esteemed among men but are an abomination in the sight of God (Luke 16:15).

CHAPTER NINE
BABBLING IN BABYLON

Why is understanding the subject of tongues so essential for us today? I believe the modern charismatic movement was foretold in Bible prophecy.

Revelation chapter 18 tells us: "And he cried mightily with a strong voice, saying, Babylon the great is fallen, is fallen. ... And I heard another voice from heaven, saying, Come out of her, my people, that ye be not partakers of her sins, and that ye receive not of her plagues" (verses 2, 4).

We must remember that one of the principal characteristics of ancient Babylon at the tower of Babel was a confusion of tongues (Genesis 11:7–9). Revelation is telling us that in the last days, God's people are to be called out of Babylon and its confusing counterfeit religious systems.

"And I saw three unclean spirits like frogs come out of the mouth of the dragon, and out of the mouth of the beast, and out of the mouth of the false prophet" (Revelation 16:13). The phrase "out of the mouth" represents speech, and please don't miss the fact that a frog's main weapon is its tongue. Unclean tongues? Perhaps God is trying to tell us something. Remember that the confusion of tongues at Babel was not a blessing of the Spirit, but rather a curse for their rebellion. In fact, we get our modern word "babbling" from the story of ancient Babel. At Pentecost, the curse of Babel was reversed so others might understand the gospel.

Chapter Ten
Given to the Obedient

I have met people who told me they've had the baptism of the Holy Spirit because they spoke in tongues; yet they held a cigarette in one hand and a can of beer in the other. Now let's get something straight. There are some basic requirements for receiving this most precious gift of the Holy Spirit.

Jesus says, "If ye love me, keep my commandments. And I will pray the Father, and he shall give you another Comforter, that he may abide with you for ever; Even the Spirit of truth" (John 14:15–17).

"And we are his witnesses of these things; and so is also the Holy Ghost, *whom God hath given to them that obey him*" (Acts 5:32, emphasis added).

A few years ago several famous TV evangelists fell by the way. They all claimed to be filled with the Holy Spirit and have the gift of tongues. But they were living in gross immoral disobedience. They would speak in tongues on TV, then leave the studio to live a compromising life. Something just wasn't right. These men also caused me to wonder, "If this is the genuine gift of tongues, then why do these charismatic evangelists need an army of interpreters to translate for them when they preach overseas?"

Why does God give the Spirit? "But ye shall receive power, after that the Holy Ghost is come upon you: and ye shall be witnesses unto me" (Acts 1:8). God does not give us the Spirit to babble, but as power for witnessing!

How can we receive the genuine gift of the Holy Spirit? Totally submit to God, be willing to forgive others, obey Him, and *ask*. Luke 11:13 says, "If ye then, being evil, know how to give good gifts unto your children: how much more shall your heavenly Father give the Holy Spirit to them that ask him?"

---

[1] *The Concise Columbia Encyclopedia* and *Compton's Interactive Encyclopedia*, under the entry "Delphi."

[2] *Compton's Interactive Encyclopedia*, under the entry "Pentecostals."